Assignment Complete

Caregiving, Loss, and Learning to Live Again

Gwendolyn Keyes Baker, MA

In Loving Memory

"Honor your father and your mother. Then you will live a
long, full life
in the land the Lord your God is giving you."
Exodus 20:12 (NLT)

This book is dedicated in loving memory of my parents
who showed us what it meant to live with grace and
dignity:
Walter Keyes, Jr. (2024)
Alethia Smalls Keyes (2026)

And in honor of my aunties, my mom's sisters whom she
loved and missed greatly:
Ordell Smalls Walker (2016)
Willie Mae Smalls Rivers (2024)

"Greatly Missed. Forever Loved."

Acknowledgments

While this book grew from my personal reflection and processing, I am incredibly grateful for my siblings — Pat, Dee, Rob, Pris, Sherry and Jermaine — who experienced this journey right alongside me. Each of us contributed in our own unique way, and together we fulfilled the promise we made to our parents. It wasn't easy, but we did it! I love and appreciate each of you.

On behalf of our family, heartfelt thanks to the aides, nurses, hospice staff, and other professionals who supported our family along the way. Your guidance, patience, and kindness helped us navigate a challenging and unfamiliar season.

I am also deeply grateful to Penny Rogers, Monica Washington-Speaks, Marion Kelly, Natalie Bowers Miller, Trevette Wallace-Hall, Valencia Bowers Mouzon, and Chantea Williams — an amazing group of beta readers who gave their time and honest feedback to help enhance this resource.

Most of all, I thank God for the opportunity and the strength to care for our parents. It was both a responsibility and an honor, and their legacy now continues in the lives of those of us who loved them dearly.

For every caregiver currently serving, be encouraged. I'm praying for you.

To every caregiver who gave their best and is now on the other side — job well done.

Contents

A Note Before You Begin

"The fact that you showed up — in whatever way you were able — says something important about who you are."

Caregiving doesn't look the same for everyone. Like us, some families care for loved ones at home. Others provide support from a distance — managing appointments, finances, and decisions across miles. And sometimes, the most loving choice is placing a parent or loved one in a facility equipped to provide the level of care they need and deserve.

All of it counts.

I also know that caregiving doesn't always come from a simple place. Some of you may be caring for a parent or loved one with whom your relationship has been complicated. The history may be difficult. The emotions may be mixed. And showing up anyway, even when it isn't easy, is its own kind of courage.

No matter *what* your journey looks like, this book was written with you in mind.

You may not see your exact experience reflected on every page. But my hope is that somewhere within these reflections, you'll find something that resonates — a moment of recognition, an encouragement you needed, or simply a reminder that what you're doing matters.

Caregiving is rarely, if ever, perfect.

But the fact that you showed up, in whatever way you were able, says something remarkable about who you are.

And *that* deserves to be honored.

The Silence

"Caregiving changes us. And learning how to live again after it ends is part of the journey, too."

Today makes exactly two weeks since Mom quietly slipped away, and one week since her funeral. For years, my life had run on a quiet alert system. Even when I slept, part of me was still listening. And in one day… that all ended.

We'd kept our promise and done as our parents asked. My siblings and I stepped into an assignment that was, at times, quite overwhelming. In spite of that, we successfully cared for not one but two parents in their nineties.

It wasn't easy. We are all senior citizens too, but by God's grace we stayed the course. Some of us literally left our own homes empty for weeks at a time as we committed ourselves to caregiving.

We sacrificed work, time with our own families, church involvement, and vacations. Every aspect of our lives had to be centered around our caregiving responsibilities.

With both parents now gone, we have time. Freedom to do things we weren't able to do before. But in reality, I'm feeling a bit lost. And I'm sure some of my siblings do, too.

I no longer need to Facetime mom to check in. And, there's no longer a reason to travel every other week to spend time with her. Truth be told, I'm struggling with the silence that has taken over the house and my life.

Her room is empty. There's no need to ensure her favorites – raisin bread and the individual bottles of Simply Orange juice are stocked. There are no wrappers rattling through the monitor, startling me in the early morning hours as she unwraps and eats Lifesaver mints. No more hearing her and my sister giggle about gossiping and telling yies (lies). No need to check the camera from my home if the doorbell rings after a certain hour. Because there's no longer a need for the nurse, aide, or chaplain.

I expected a sense of calm and relief. Instead, there's silence and a void. And the silence is, honestly, *deafening*.

Because caregiving had become my life on so many levels, I actually feel a bit disoriented. That first week I found myself in a daze, watching video clips of mom— over and over again just to hear her voice. To hear her speak Gullah-Geechie. And of course, to hear her say, 'I didn't do all they said, but I did some' — as only she could. I looked at pictures from the funeral, just trying to wrap my mind around the fact that she is *really* gone.

Before now caregiving had its own silences. The long hours while mom slept. Being tied to the monitor while life outside kept moving. Sitting in the same room with her, present but unable to do much of anything except provide her some company. You learn to sit with that kind of quiet.

But *this* silence…. it's different.

This is the silence that comes after the assignment has ended.

What do those of us who have given ourselves so fully to the care of our loved ones do now? How do we find closure…..if there's such a thing?

What do we do with the silence of this new season?

That's the question.

Over the past few years, my siblings and I have learned a great deal about caregiving—often through trial and error. Much of what we learned came in real time as we simply tried to do the next right thing for our parents.

We had no roadmap. We didn't have many conversations with others who had already walked this road. Even some of the doctors had no answers or guidance. In many ways, we were learning on the fly.

Now, standing in the quiet that follows, I realize there are lessons from our journey that may help others who are still in the middle of caregiving. Or, those who may one day find themselves there.

Caregiving has seasons filled with activity and responsibility. Seasons marked by waiting, watching, and learning to accept changes we can't control. And eventually there is the moment when the caregiving ends, and we are left to process what caregiving asked of us, what we learned along the way, and how we will forge a path forward.

This book isn't meant to be a manual with perfect answers. Instead, it's simply a reflection guide, an act of love designed to help others.

If you're currently caring for someone you love, my hope is that these pages will help you navigate the journey with greater clarity, grace, and peace. And if you're standing in the quiet that comes afterward like we are, perhaps these reflections will help give language to the roller coaster of emotions that are sometimes overwhelming and difficult to articulate.

Because caregiving changes us.

And learning how to live again after it ends is also part of the journey.

CHAPTER ONE

When Caregiving Finds You

"Somewhere along the way, you become more than a son or daughter. You become an advocate."

Caregiver.

It's a word many of us probably never give much thought to until one day it quietly becomes a part of our lives.

As I now stand in the silence that follows an extended season of caregiving, I find myself looking back on how the journey began. For most families, the answer is simple and similar to mine: it didn't start all at once.

Caregiving rarely announces itself with a clear beginning. More often, it enters gradually, through small changes that are easy to overlook at first.

I understand now what a caregiver really is — simply someone who begins taking responsibility for helping another person live safely and with dignity when they can no longer manage life independently.

Years ago, I wouldn't have given much thought to the role of caregiver. My maternal grandparents died young, and while my paternal grandparents passed away during my young adulthood, I had no responsibility for their care over an extended period of time.

Sure, I knew my parents would grow older. That's a part of life. But knowing that in theory is very different from understanding what it could *actually* mean.

For most of my adult life, my parents were strong and independent. Active, involved, and fully engaged in life. So, the idea that they might one day need significant care never seriously crossed my mind.

In retrospect, I now realize how common that probably is — especially as we continue to see people living longer than ever before. What a wonderful gift that is! But longer lives also mean families must prepare themselves for decisions and responsibilities they likely never considered.

Life was moving along as usual. Mom, in particular, traveled, served in her church and community, spent time with grandchildren, and enjoyed the simple things that make life full. Nothing about those moments remotely suggested that change was on the horizon.

Those changes are likely noticed first by someone who happens to spend more time nearby. In many families, a person who sees the parent more frequently begins to notice what appears to be small changes. For us, that was my sister who landed a job in our hometown and stayed at our parents' home during the workweek.

Those early observations can lead to simple conversations within the family.

"Have you noticed...?" "I'm not sure if this is anything, but..."

Those conversations may then prompt everyone to pay closer attention.

Families then begin doing what comes naturally. Helping wherever they can.

Someone might remind a parent about bills. Someone else might stop by a little more often just to check in. Visits may become a little longer. Phone calls become a little more frequent.

At this point though, most families still aren't thinking in terms of caregiving. Everyone is managing their own responsibilities. Nothing is formally organized. No one sits down to divide tasks or create a plan. Family members just step in where needed.

At first, it just feels like helping the people who once helped us — just a little more often.

Those changes are likely signaling a shift; yet, life may continue much as it always has. Helping a parent or loved one becomes something that just fits in around everything else.

Over time, though, small adjustments become necessary.

Schedules require a little more coordination. Errands are sometimes planned around a visit to the house.

Practical matters begin to require more attention as well. The reminder about bills might now move to actually writing checks and mailing monthly bills. Cleaning or repairs around the house may need to be handled. Help to ensure that they don't skip meals. Small things that now require someone to keep an eye on them.

Medical appointments may begin to enter the picture, too. A visit to the doctor here. A conversation about medications there. Nothing unusual for someone growing older, but enough to make the family take notice.

Even then, it still doesn't feel unusual.

It just feels like family helping where necessary. And most of us probably think of it that way.

Helping.

Not caregiving.

It's clear now that we were slowly learning more about what our parents needed, doing what seemed right in the moment.

Without a formal conversation or plan, you step forward. You ask questions, help with decisions, and pay attention to things that once belonged fully to your parents. Somewhere along the way, though, you become more than a son or daughter. You become an advocate.

And whether you planned for it or not, caregiving has found you – perhaps before you even realized it.

For so many families, the role arrives without instructions. We find ourselves learning as we go — figuring out responsibilities, navigating family dynamics, and making decisions we never imagined we'd have to make.

That's our story, and it's probably yours, too.

As the journey progressed, caregiving really required the best of me — even on days I felt I had very little left to give. It required patience, self-discipline, tough skin, and sometimes the courage to make decisions that were neither understood nor appreciated in the moment.

I won't pretend we did it in our own strength. Faith was the foundation that held us. Prayer, the Word, and honest conversations with God about where I was — mentally, emotionally, physically, spiritually — is what kept me showing up. God was my very Present Help in the assignment so I didn't have to carry it alone.

My siblings and I made it through sacrifice and teamwork, with each of us contributing in the ways we could. There were moments of great laughter, both of our parents were hilarious, and moments when we quietly grieved as we watched the changes unfold before our eyes.

But we loved and served them well. We cared for them, and did our best to honor their wishes and preserve their dignity. And in that, I find great peace.

I realize that many families are probably in that stage right now — helping more often, paying closer attention, but not yet realizing that caregiving may be secretly taking shape. Not yet realizing just how quickly things can change.

For many families, the realization comes suddenly — often through a moment that makes it crystal clear that something has *truly* changed.

CHAPTER TWO

The Moment Everything Changes

*"Small signs of confusion or disorientation should
never be ignored."*

For a while, helping feels manageable. Yes. Life is different, but it still feels familiar.

Then something happens that changes everything.

Most caregiving journeys likely have a moment like this. It may not seem dramatic to anyone outside the family, but for those closest to the situation, it becomes a moment you don't forget.

A parent or loved one's hygiene may change. Small things might be forgotten — like eating consistent meals.

Sometimes it's a phone call late at night. Or a situation where a parent becomes confused or disoriented. Sometimes it's a fall, a medical concern, or something that simply just seems off.

Whatever the circumstance, it gets everyone's attention — and the questions change.

Is mom safe at home alone? Should someone be checking on dad more often? Are we seeing changes that we didn't fully recognize before? Or, that we now recognize as more serious?

In many families, this is the moment when helping turns into caregiving. And, it can look very differently in each situation.

I can very vividly remember the incident that triggered the necessity of 24-hour care for our parents. The need to ensure their safety. The moment that literally changed the course of our lives for a few years.

One evening mom woke up disoriented and felt that she had to get out of the house. They live on a very busy road and it was late at night. She was in danger, but thank God He had her covered. Dad alerted our neighbor — who always kept an eye on our parents. He then called 911. A highway patrolman noticed her, and our neighbor helped identify and get her to safety. Then, the neighbor contacted us. That night literally shook our world and set us on a quest for answers.

We learned that situations like that aren't uncommon in older adults. They can happen suddenly and for many reasons ranging from an infection such as a urinary tract infection (UTI), to something more serious like the gradual development of cognitive decline or dementia.

Whatever the cause, these moments remind families of something important: when changes begin to appear, pay attention.

Across the country there are increasing reports of missing seniors — some found safely, others not. My heart aches every time I see a post or news report. And I find myself praying often for seniors and their families because I know the journey. And most importantly, I know that small signs of confusion or disorientation should never be ignored.

On that note, because early signs can be so subtle, increased awareness may help other families avoid a similar experience. Let me briefly share a few signs families should be sure to give attention to.

A parent may begin sleeping more than usual or seem unusually tired throughout the day. Routine tasks — paying bills on time, turning off the stove, finishing something around the house like laundry — may start slipping.

Confusion about time or place is another sign. So are personality or mood shifts including things like unusual sadness, irritability, or withdrawal from things they once enjoyed.

And wandering or disorientation, both inside and outside the home, should never be dismissed as just getting older.

If you're noticing any of these, please pay close attention. What you're seeing may mean that it's time to begin in-depth conversations with family members and medical professionals.

Sometimes the cause can be something temporary, such as a UTI, dehydration, or a medication issue. Other times it may signal a deeper change that requires additional care and attention. Paying attention can help families respond early, and with wisdom, patience, and dignity.

For our family, that night marked the beginning of a deeper awareness. It prompted conversations we had not yet been ready to have and decisions we had not yet planned to make.

Caregiving had arrived — not quietly but abruptly — and taking responsibility couldn't wait.

Beyond the practical decisions that suddenly need to be made, these situations can also trigger different emotions and challenges all at the same time.

Of course, there is grave concern for the parent or loved one, and uncertainty about what the future now holds.

And sometimes there is even tension within the family as everyone tries to understand what must happen next.

Each person processes the situation differently.

Some family members may feel a strong sense of urgency. Others may struggle to accept that things are really changing. Still others may worry about how caregiving will affect their work, finances, or families.

All of these reactions are real and they're normal.

Caregiving does not unfold in neat or predictable ways.

Families often find themselves navigating not only the needs of an aging parent or loved one, but also the emotions, perspectives, and practical realities of multiple siblings and other close relatives.

And in many situations, responsibilities will not fall evenly.

Sometimes distance plays a role. Sometimes work schedules, family obligations, or personal health limit what some people can do. Caregiving also requires skills and temperaments that may not be a strength for some people.

Funny story. We had an emergency at mom's (more about the situation comes later), and we had to move quickly. I was helping mom; my brother was helping dad. The other sibling, who shall remain unnamed, was to call 911. About 15 minutes later this unnamed individual asked, 'Has anyone called 911?' Later as we all laughed about it, this individual said, 'I don't do well in crisis. I went outside and ran around in circles.' Now we know.

As a result, a smaller number of family members often carry a larger share of the day-to-day responsibility.

That reality alone can be challenging.

It can create fatigue and financial strain. And at times, it can even create misunderstandings within the family.

But it's also where many caregivers rise to the moment of leadership.

Someone begins asking questions and gathering information. Someone else begins coordinating what needs to happen next.

Oftentimes that leadership isn't formally assigned.

It simply emerges.

Because someone recognized the need and was willing to step forward.

I've come to realize that moments like this mark an important turning point in the caregiving journey. They're the moments when families begin to see the situation more clearly. The moments when helping gradually becomes responsibility.

And almost without anyone planning it, someone begins to lead.

CHAPTER THREE

When Roles Begin to Shift

"Without much discussion, the family naturally begins looking to that person — even though he or she has no desire to be 'the one.'"

In many families, there's already someone who tends to organize things — the one who plans gatherings, keeps people connected, and steps in when the family needs to figure a situation out.

When caregiving begins, those same patterns often continue. Without much discussion, the family naturally begins looking to that person even though he or she has no desire to be "the one." I can remember a few people essentially telling me was the one.

It can feel heavy, and really, quite uncomfortable. And sometimes, you can feel misunderstood. The responsibility. The constant decision-making. The emotional strain. It can look glamourous if you don't really understand the weight of the assignment.

And over time, it can feel… lonely.

But I've seen first-hand that certain qualities make a huge difference during difficult seasons, or in delicate situations.

The ability to stay calm in a crisis or when emotions are high. The willingness to listen to different perspectives, try to see all sides, and mediate difficult conversations. The discipline to focus on what needs to be done and not worry about who gets the credit. And sometimes, the courage to say what needs to be said — especially when it isn't popular.

Caregiving can put a lot of pressure on families, and require difficult decisions you never imagined having to make.

As our parents aged, there came a time when keeping their lives peaceful became a priority. And in order to do that, we had to decide what to share — and what to keep.

There were things we chose not to tell mom, in particular. We weren't intentionally hiding things from her, but weighed the options given where she was mentally, emotionally, and physically at the time.

I remember my sisters and I having a discussion about whether or not we'd tell her about one of her cousins who passed. They were pretty close and spoke fairly often at one time. It was a really tough decision, but we ultimately decided that telling her wasn't in her best interest at that time. She'd been having some down days and we didn't want to add to it. We were so uncomfortable whenever she'd mention her cousin's name, and the fact that they hadn't spoken in some time. I just *knew* that she was going to ask us to call her at some point. How in the world would we explain our decision not to tell her that she'd died?! Fortunately, she never asked and we never told her.

That's just one scenario, but we faced others. In each case, we made the decision carefully, together, and always with her best interest at heart.

Caregiving will sometimes require you to make decisions that aren't easy to explain. But when those decisions are rooted in love, wisdom, and protecting their peace, they matter.

Everyone loves the parent or relative involved, and wants the best outcome. But love doesn't always translate into agreement.

In every family there are different perspectives, different capacities, and different realities. And sometimes, those differences create tension.

Even when everyone wants the same *outcome*, there can be very different opinions about how to get there.

What is best? What is necessary? What is realistic?

When these come together under pressure, they don't always blend easily.

And for the person handling much of the day-to-day responsibility, that can feel especially heavy — because it's not just the care itself. It's the weight of decisions. The weight of communication. The responsibility of trying to keep everyone informed and, at times, aligned.

Truthfully, there are moments of frustration. Moments when you feel unsupported. Moments when it seems like others don't fully understand what it takes to carry this role every day.

Those feelings don't make you a bad caregiver. They make you human.

Caregiving places families in situations they were never trained for. There is no guidebook for how to navigate the decisions, conversations, or emotions that come with it. For those reasons, families don't always get it right.

And when that happens, grace is required.

Grace for one another. Grace for the different ways people show up. Grace for what others may not fully understand. And grace for yourself.

Holding a family together during caregiving doesn't mean everything runs smoothly or that everyone always agrees.

It means continuing to choose, even when it's hard, to stay focused on the care, safety, and dignity of your loved one.

Sometimes that means having difficult conversations. Sometimes it means setting boundaries. And sometimes, it means silently continuing to do what needs to be done — despite the challenges that come with it.

Many families eventually find their way.

Support may not always look the way you expected in the beginning, but it can grow. Understanding can deepen. And roles can become clearer.

And even though the journey isn't perfect, progress is still possible.

Because at the center of it all is something that remains constant.

Love.

And when love stays at the center, it gives families a way to keep moving forward — even in those weighty, difficult moments.

CHAPTER FOUR

The Weight Caregivers Carry

"Receiving help isn't weakness. It's wisdom that helps ensure care continues in a sustainable way."

As caregiving deepens, responsibilities grow heavier.

Over time, it begins to shape everyday life. Caregiving can literally become the filter through which almost every decision is made.

A quick trip to the store may need to be planned around whether someone else is at home. Work schedules may need to be adjusted, sometimes to the point of stepping away from work altogether.

Some caregivers even find themselves balancing two households. Their own home needs attention. Spouses still need and deserve attention. Bills still need to be paid. Truth is, responsibilities to work and family don't disappear just because caregiving has entered the picture.

These are what I often call the *hidden* costs of caregiving.

They're not just financial, though those can be significant.

They're emotional. Mental. Physical. Relational.

Caregiving costs time, sleep, energy, and flexibility. It can mean lost income, and significant strain on relationships.

When the full weight of caregiving is not recognized, it becomes easy to assume that more can be done… that what's currently being done isn't enough. And sometimes, without realizing it, others place additional expectations on the very ones already carrying the most.

Caregiving isn't a small responsibility. It's a significant, ongoing commitment.

As we cared for our parents, I remember people often telling us how blessed we were. And make no mistake—we absolutely were. It was a compliment, and they meant well.

But there were moments when it made me feel a way.

Because can you see my fatigue?

Feel my discouragement?

Did they understand? Maybe. Probably.

But simply acknowledging it would have said, "I see you."

And sometimes, being seen is enough to help you keep going.

I remember one of the last Sundays I was able to get mom out to church—for a 10 a.m. service mind you.

I got up early to get myself partially ready, then managed to get her up, bathed, fed, dressed, and out for church. That was no small task to accomplish alone. I was exhausted by the time we got there.

But I can still very vividly remember one of the ladies coming over to greet mom. She also reached over, gently touched my hand, and mouthed a word of encouragement to me.

It touched my heart. That small, simple act reminded me of the God who sees.

In that moment, I knew that not only did *she* see me—but God did too. And it gave me the lift that I needed.

That moment has stayed with me. And it also reminded me of something important.

If you know someone who is caring for a loved one, never underestimate the power of simply acknowledging them.

A kind word. A gentle touch. A sincere moment of connection.

Sometimes it may be as simple as asking, "How are you… *really?*"

Not in passing. But with intention.

Now, I understand that this can be sensitive. Not everyone is ready to open up, and not every moment is the right moment. That's where discernment comes in.

But even if a caregiver doesn't say much, the question alone communicates something powerful — "I see you."

Feeling weary doesn't mean we don't care.

It means we are feeling the impact of what we've likely been carrying for a while.

There are moments when we feel tired, overwhelmed, and even a little frustrated. And patience must be renewed constantly.

Those feelings can be difficult to admit.

They may even carry some guilt, because many caregivers believe they should always feel patient and strong. But caregiving is demanding work, and honest emotions are part of the experience.

There were also moments when I had to step back and give attention to myself—to take care of me in the middle of caregiving.

I had to get creative, because what I needed wasn't always readily available.

Sometimes that meant resting when my parents rested. I would take naps when they did, keeping a monitor nearby so I could hear movement or if they called me.

Other times, it meant using things that made life a little easier—like ordering groceries when I couldn't get out.

Adding internet to their home helped me stay connected to parts of my life that mattered like joining Bible study online, or watching services when I couldn't attend in person.

It also allowed me to bring moments of enjoyment to them—music they loved or a movie they might enjoy when they felt like being a little more engaged.

None of these things removed the responsibility.

But they helped lighten the load a little.

And sometimes, small adjustments like these can make a big difference.

Caregiving doesn't require perfection, but it does require wisdom. And sometimes that wisdom looks like finding simple ways to keep going.

Caregiving requires a great deal, and we have to acknowledge that we can't do everything on our own.

We need help.

And that support may need to come from outside the family.

For our family, that meant exploring available resources.

I applied for and received caregiver grants that helped support the care we were providing. Having someone come in to bathe them while we prepared breakfast or to strip and re-make the bed was a huge blessing.

We also learned about options like respite care or time set aside to give caregivers a needed break. You can have help come in or your loved one can go to a facility.

Truthfully, outside help isn't always welcomed—even when it's needed.

Caregiving can be sensitive for families. Some want privacy. The care recipient may not want strangers to see them in such a vulnerable state.

So, like us, you may need to have hard conversations and work through those challenges in order to get what you need. You can also plan tasks for the aides that limit their time with your loved one until they become more comfortable.

These kinds of resources can be really helpful. But the challenge is that many families don't know where to start, and sometimes the information isn't readily offered.

We found that some medical providers couldn't guide us to what was available.

So, I had to do the work.

Ask the questions. Do the research. Reach out to local agencies or organizations that support caregivers. Follow up with them if you have to.

Yes, I know.

It's one more thing added to your plate, and you may not feel up for it nor have time for it.

But if you can find the strength to push forward, it may be well worth the effort.

Go on a little virtual hunting expedition and see what resources may be available to you.

Support is out there.

And please understand that receiving help isn't weakness.

It's wisdom that helps ensure that care continues in a sustainable way.

That being said, spiritual support is equally important.

For me, prayer was not optional—it was necessary.

Scripture, even if it was just one verse, became a place of encouragement and guidance.

Faith reminded me that honoring our parents is not only a family responsibility, but also a spiritual calling.

And *that* understanding gave me strength on days when the path felt long and difficult.

At the same time, it's important to remember something else.

The person receiving care is also walking through this experience.

Aging, illness, or disability isn't something people choose. It's the hand life deals, and they're learning how to live with it too.

For many, that means a loss of independence.

Things that were once easy for them now require help. Decisions may no longer be theirs alone. Even the simplest routines can begin to change.

And that isn't always easy to accept.

Moments of frustration, sadness, and other emotions may come out in ways that are difficult to understand.

Sometimes it may look like resistance, sound like irritation or anger, and at times it may even feel personal.

Most often, it isn't.

It's the weight of what they're experiencing and the reality of needing help.

Remembering that can make a difference—and add understanding.

And sometimes, that understanding helps us respond with a little more patience, a little more grace, and a little more compassion in the moments it's needed most.

Because caregiving asks a lot of everyone, including the one in the center of it all.

CHAPTER FIVE

Holding the Family Together

"Unity in caregiving doesn't happen automatically. It is something that must be chosen — repeatedly."

Have you noticed that things don't feel quite as simple as they once did?

As caregiving continues, it's not just the responsibilities that increase. Relationships can begin to feel more strained as well.

Family members can be in the same room, having the same conversation—and still walk away with completely different understandings of what was discussed or of what just happened.

One person is thinking about what needs to be done right now.

Another is thinking about what this will look like long-term.

And someone else may still be trying to process how things changed so quickly.

That's often how differences begin to surface.

And if we're not intentional, those differences can create friction.

Caregiving doesn't just require effort in what we do—it requires care in how we relate to one another.

Good communication becomes even more essential.

Some people are comfortable talking through anything.

Others find it difficult to engage in hard conversations.

And when communication breaks down, tension doesn't disappear. It builds.

Sometimes silently beneath the surface.

Until it shows up later… often at the most inopportune time.

That's why caregiving requires intentional, consistent and healthy communication.

About tasks—but also about expectations.

About decisions.

About how each person is experiencing the journey.

And, when appropriate, also with the person *receiving* care.

Because their voice matters too.

Another challenge families often face is how differently people respond to change.

As parents and loved ones age or face illness, some family members accept the reality quickly and begin preparing for what's next.

Others need time.

Time to process.

Time to accept a diagnosis.

Time to adjust to what it all means.

And in that space, differences can grow.

There may be disagreement about treatment decisions.

About medications.

About how much intervention is needed—or not needed.

Each person is responding from their own perspective.

And the different perspectives don't always line up.

There are also moments when it may feel like one person is doing more than everyone else.

Sometimes that feeling reflects reality.

Other times, it reflects what isn't fully seen.

And sometimes, people *want* to do more—but simply can't.

Without clarity, these differences can easily lead to frustration.

Having multiple children in a family can be a blessing.

But it can also introduce complexity.

Some families organize, communicate, and work well together.

Others struggle to find that rhythm.

At times, people may begin to separate into sides.

Conversations may become strained.

And division can easily take root.

Love is still there, but alignment doesn't always follow.

And navigating this season requires more than love alone.

It requires intention.

It requires humility.

It requires the ability to think beyond our own perspective and consider what others may be carrying.

In that space, families need someone willing to stay in the room — not to have all the answers, but to keep the conversation moving in the right direction.

Someone who can bring clarity and calm when emotions are high.

Someone who can help the family stay focused on what matters most.

Because challenges will come.

And how those moments are handled will shape what the experience becomes.

For many families, caregiving means spending more time together than they have in years—sometimes even since childhood.

And that alone can be an adjustment.

For us, that became true in a way we never anticipated.

A squirrel caused an electrical fire at my parents' home, and just like that, we found ourselves moving them, their equipment, and our belongings into an Airbnb for four months while renovations were completed. Four of us living under one roof, caring for aging parents, while my brother and I simultaneously oversaw the renovations, the shopping, and everything else that comes with resetting a home.

And I had to share a room with my sister.

In twin beds.

I was accustomed to sleeping in my king size bed, and a twin bed wasn't in my plans. Every time I turned over, I was convinced the floor was coming for me.

My brothers had their own name for them.

Prison cots.

And honestly? That seemed on point.

Now imagine this: four senior citizens, who are used to living alone, caring for their aging parents while all living together under one roof.

Some days we laughed and had the best time.

And some days? I will just say that there were other not-so-fun emotions present. As an introvert, I needed my personal space and quiet moments. *Desperately.*

The point is, proximity is its own kind of pressure. Even among people who love each other deeply.

Different routines.

Different personalities.

Different ways of living.

Some people stay up late.

Others rise early.

Some are quiet.

Others are more expressive.

All of those differences come into the same space.

And they don't stay theoretical—they show up in real time.

In conversations that don't quite land the way they were intended.

In decisions that take longer than expected.

In moments where patience is stretched.

And at times like these, how we respond to one another matters - to caring well, to supporting one another, and to moving through that season in a way that preserves both the well-being of your loved one and the relationships within the family.

What matters isn't who is right—but how we choose to move forward together.

This is where grace becomes essential.

The kind of grace that allows room for differences.

The kind that resists quick judgment.

And the kind that recognizes that not everything is fully understood in the moment.

But grace alone isn't always enough.

There are also times when boundaries are needed.

Boundaries that protect what is sustainable.

Boundaries that bring clarity where expectations may be unclear.

And boundaries that help ensure one person is not carrying more than they can reasonably hold.

Boundaries aren't about pushing people away.

They're about making it possible to continue caring well—without becoming overwhelmed or depleted.

When grace and boundaries work together, they create space for healthier relationships in the middle of a very demanding season.

And that matters.

Because unity in caregiving doesn't happen automatically.

It's not something families can assume will just fall into place. It is something that must be chosen—repeatedly.

Chosen in conversations. Chosen in moments of tension. Chosen when it would be easier to withdraw or shut down.

It doesn't mean everything will be perfect. But choosing it repeatedly — in the hard moments, in the quiet ones — is what holds a family together.

CHAPTER SIX

Finishing Well

"Caregiving is not only about walking through loss. It is also about recognizing life — while it is still unfolding in front of you."

There comes a point in the caregiving journey when you begin to sense that things are changing…..again.

Not in small ways, but in ways that feel more final.

The needs may increase. The pace may slow. And everything begins to feel different.

More intentional.

More sacred.

Because somewhere within you, there is an awareness that this season is coming to a close.

Finishing well doesn't happen by accident.

It requires presence. Tenderness. A willingness to lean into parts of the journey that aren't always easy.

In this stage, care often becomes quieter. Less about doing. More about being.

Being present.

Being attentive.

Being willing to sit in spaces that don't always require words.

You begin to recognize that time is no longer something to manage—it is something to honor.

Every conversation matters.

Every touch matters.

Everything carries meaning in a way it didn't before.

So, you show up…intentionally.

For our family, finishing well also meant choosing to celebrate along the way. Even as we were navigating the reality of what was unfolding.

And those expressions didn't only happen at the end. We learned to recognize and celebrate the smaller wins too.

On days when she ate well after not wanting to eat at all.

On days she felt strong enough to come out of her room.

On days she'd want to sit in the doorway and quietly watch the cars pass by… and the people going about their day.

Those may seem small to someone else. But to us, they were significant. They were reminders that even in a season of decline, there was still life to acknowledge.

Still reasons to celebrate.

Because caregiving isn't only about walking through loss. It's also about recognizing life while it's still unfolding in front of you.

And sometimes, life shows up in the most unexpected ways.

About two weeks before she passed away, mom woke up early…. which wasn't the norm, and announced that she was going to the store.

No. She didn't ask for someone to go *for* her.

She wanted to go shop for herself.

Despite my sisters' efforts, there was no convincing her otherwise. And by that point in the journey, we'd learned to acquiesce in such moments. Trying to talk her out of something she was determined to do only created frustration, and she deserved better.

At this stage, most things required two people. A simple store run was no small undertaking. But my sisters got themselves together, got mom dressed, and off they went.

What an adventure they had!

The store had a special cart where she could sit facing them as they pushed her through the aisles. People throughout the store were drawn to her — smiling, stopping, showing her love and attention. She was out. She was present. And she was thoroughly in her element.

But then came the prices.

Mom had always been frugal. And it had been quite some time since she'd done her own grocery shopping. So, the cost of everything was, let's just say… a surprise to her. I'm sure my sisters were probably a little bit embarrassed because she can't whisper. A little aside here. We were in church one Sunday and she told me something to which I replied, 'mom, you can't whisper. She replied with her usual quick wit, 'I ain't trying.' She really was quite the character.

Anyway, after all of that — the early morning determination, the getting dressed, the special cart, her fan club throughout the store, and the sticker shock —

She shopped for…. boiled peanuts.

Yes. Boiled peanuts.

When my sister told me about it, we laughed. And we still laugh.

But here's what we also know now.

That trip — that simple, unplanned, slightly chaotic trip to the store — was her last interaction with people outside of her family, in her community.

She didn't know that. We didn't know that.

But she got to go out on her own terms, surrounded by people who were intrigued by her, doing something that made her feel like herself.

That's no small thing.

That's finishing well. And, I honor my sisters for showing up so beautifully in that moment…. because I *fully* understand what it took to make that happen.

As you can see, mom was large and in charge until the end.

My last visit with her, I sat beside her bed and helped her eat some of those peanuts.

Then, in honor of what would've been her 93rd birthday, we celebrated — even in her absence.

But there was cake. And balloons.

Sparkling cider.

Glasses raised in honor of a woman who enjoyed those simple things.

It wasn't elaborate. But it was heartfelt.

Because her life was worth celebrating, not just *remembering.*

There were difficult days in that final season.

Hard decisions to make.

Emotions that sat close to the surface.

And times when strength had to be drawn from a deeper place.

But even in that, there was clarity. We understood what mattered.

We understood the assignment.

And we remained committed to finishing it well.

One of the most sacred experiences for me came at the end.

After the viewing.

After others had shared their final goodbyes.

There was a quiet space.

Set apart. Just for us.

A time to say goodbye in a way that felt deeply personal.

We gently prepared her.....pulling up the soft lining surrounding her.

Tucking her neatly into it.

Covering her with care and love.

One final opportunity to care for the woman who had *sacrificially* cared for us.

And then… we closed the casket.

Slowly.

Intentionally.

With full awareness of what that meant.

There was no rush.

No distraction.

Just presence.

It was sacred.

And then, we made a decision.

To honor her life the way she deserved — with worship, with singing, with gratitude, and with all who had come to join us in celebrating her life.

Because while there was grief, there was also peace.

Peace in knowing that we had done all we could.

Peace in knowing that we had shown up.

Peace in knowing that we'd loved her well.

And that continued even after the service was over.

After we'd laid her to rest.

After the formalities were complete.

We gathered again. At mom's house.

And we watched a slideshow of pictures and video clips from her life.

Oh the memories.

The moments.

And at the end, there was a clip of her walking down the hallway with her walker.

When she reached the doorway to her room, she paused.

Then turned slightly… looking back.

It was a simple moment.

But in that space, watching a video recorded months earlier, it felt like more.

As if she was saying goodbye. I'll see y'all in the morning.

Finishing well doesn't mean the journey was easy.

It certainly doesn't mean there were no hard days.

It means that, in the end, you can look back and know that you were present.

That you gave all you had.

That you honored the life of the one you were entrusted to care for.

Caregiving asks a lot.

But it also gives something in return.

Perspective. Depth. A deeper understanding of love in action.

And when the journey comes to an end, what remains is not just what was lost —

but what was built along the way.

The memories. The moments. The quiet knowing that you fulfilled something special.

And when I look back now, I can say this with peace:

We did it.

We showed up.

We loved our parents well.

And now…

Our assignment is complete.

Learning to Live Again

"And when you're ready… Live."

When caregiving ends, the responsibility may be over — but the adjustment is just beginning.

For a long time, life was shaped around what needed to be done. What once required our attention, our energy, our presence no longer does. And while there may be a sense of freedom in that, there can also be an unfamiliar space that feels both freeing and unsettling at the same time.

Caregiving changes us. In many ways. And when the assignment ends, it can also change the way we see ourselves.

The routines that once structured our days are gone. And now, we're left with a question that doesn't always have a quick answer:

Who am I now? How do I live in this new reality and new season?

That's part of this transition. And it's a real one.

There's no right way to move through it. No timeline that says when you should feel "better." No expectation that you should immediately know what life looks like next.

I'm new in this space and, honestly, I don't have all the answers. But what I'm discovering as I process this loss is that this isn't a season to rush into what's next. It's a season to gently rediscover what remains and what's ready to emerge.

It's a season to give myself permission to rest. To feel. And to find my way. In time.

Writing this book has been one step for me. And like you, I am still learning what next looks like.

It's different for each of us, but a few things have helped me as I begin to move forward. I don't share these as steps you must follow, just anchors that have helped hold me in what feels so unstable right now.

Before deciding what's next, I've had to give myself permission to sit in where I am. This moment, as unfamiliar as it feels, deserves your attention too.

I've also had to pay attention to what is still alive in me. Not everything ended with caregiving or loss. There are still things that stir my heart — small sparks of curiosity, moments of peace, and I'm learning to follow those quietly.

Simple rhythms have helped more than I expected. Not grand plans or new purposes — just small, consistent, life-giving routines that have slowly begun to shape what comes next.

And I'm learning to let clarity unfold over time rather than forcing it. It rarely comes all at once. It comes as we live.

There's another layer to this transition that isn't always spoken out loud.

For many, caregiving is tied to the care of a parent. In our case, it was both parents. And when that season ends with the loss of one, and certainly both, something even deeper can shift.

It's not only the role that changes. It can feel as though a part of your identity has shifted as well. For 65 years of my life, I had two parents. And within two years, I've lost both. I was someone's child. Someone who could go home. Someone who had a living point of reference.

And now, while the love remains, the way that relationship is experienced has completely changed.

It's normal to feel uncovered in this space, to quietly question who you are *now*.

But identity doesn't disappear in this season. It shifts. What was given to us, the values, the lessons, the ways of loving and showing up — it all remains. It just lives within us now rather than being reinforced around us.

In time, new layers of identity will begin to form. Not as a replacement. As a continuation.

Journaling and writing this book have reignited something in me that I haven't felt in a very long time. I'm still in the journey, so some moments have brought tears and sadness. But it has also brought laughter, joy, and an emerging sense of renewed purpose.

It's possible to feel the weight of loss and still experience moments of lightness. One doesn't cancel out the other.

I'm actually excited about what's to come. And I believe my parents would be proud.

You may not be there yet. And that's okay. Take your time and let the process play out for you.

Family also holds a unique place in this season.

There may be times when family can't hold you in the way you need. That doesn't indicate a lack of love. It's shared loss. We're all grieving. But there's still something healing about just being together.

My sisters and I are planning time together. We've already stepped away from the house — and that has been an experience of its own. Just looking at the alarm system app on my phone and seeing it set to away has been filled with emotion.

But we're going back this weekend. We're gathering at mom's to make dinner and watch movies. We may even stay up half the night — okay, some of us may not. If you know, you know! And then the next day we're taking a water taxi around the harbor. Sunshine, fresh air, historic sites — and probably memories of the last time we took mom on a tour. I still remember enjoying lunch and then deciding to take the taxi. What a beautiful time we had.

There's no agenda — just time. Moments of conversation, moments of quiet, likely some tears, and I'm sure moments of laughter. It will feel different without her, no doubt. But because of the excitement our plans have already sparked, I know it'll be something special — because we're simply together.

Time shared — whether through conversation, memory, or quiet presence — helps maintain connection as everything else shifts. Family time in this season isn't always about finding the right words. It's about sharing space. And as old routines end, new rhythms can begin to form in the simple moments together.

Friendship can also play a huge role in this season.

After giving so much of ourselves, it may feel unfamiliar to re-engage with friends. But the right friendships don't require you to perform or return to who you were before. They can offer space to talk, to be quiet, to simply be.

Sometimes it's through conversation with someone who knows us that we begin to remember who we are outside of what we've carried. In this season, friendship is less about filling time and more about restoring connections that bring a sense of normalcy back to our lives.

This is vital — because while solitude may be necessary for a moment, we can't let isolation silently settle in. And it can happen if we're not careful. Healthy relationships help keep us connected without overwhelming us.

Some relationships may deepen in this season. Others may shift. This isn't always a loss. It can be a realignment for where we are now.

I don't know everything. But here's something I do know.

Jeremiah 29:11 reminds us that the One who sustained us through the assignment hasn't stopped making plans for us. The same God who was present in our previous season is present in this one — even if it feels quieter, slower, or unfamiliar.

That plan doesn't end where one assignment ends. And the end of the assignment isn't the end of your life.

The caregiving season may be complete.

But your story isn't.

What is meant for this season will come into view — step by step, as we continue to live.

It's the beginning of learning how to live differently.

And even though their presence is no longer here in the same way, what they gave us remains.

We're not living without it.

We're learning how to live from it.

Give yourself permission to take the journey one step at a time.

And when you're ready…

Live.

A Quiet Invitation

"Sometimes, the greatest comfort is just knowing that someone else understands."

If this book has found you in the middle of your caregiving journey—or in the silence that follows—I want you to know that you are not alone.

If something here resonated with you…

If it helped you put words to what you've been feeling…

Or if you want to share your experience with someone who understands…

I invite you to reach out.

You can share your thoughts, your story, or even just a few words about where you are in your journey.

www.GwendolynKeyesBaker.com

I may not be able to respond to every message right away, but please know that every story matters.

And if this resource has been meaningful to you, feel free to share it with someone else who may need it.

Sometimes, the greatest comfort is just knowing that someone else understands.

Gwen